Big Cats on the Loose

John Townsend

Published in association with The Basic Skills Agency

Hodder & Stoughton

A MEMBER OF THE HODDER HEAD

Acknowledgements
Cover: Bruce Coleman Inc.

Photos: p iv © Bruce Coleman Inc; p5 © Nigel Brierly/Fortean Picture Library; p8 © Hulton-Deutsch Collection/Corbis; p10 © W. Perry Conway/Corbis; p18 © Tom Bakefield/Corbis; p21 © Fritz Ploking; Frank Lane Picture Agency/Corbis; p23 Kevin Schafer/Corbis

Every effort has been made to trace copyright holders of material reproduced in this book. Any rights not acknowledged will be acknowledged in subsequent printings if notice is given to the publisher.

Orders; please contact Bookpoint Ltd, 39 Milton Park, Abingdon, Oxon OX14 4TD. Telephone (44) 01235 400414, Fax: (44) 01235 400454. Lines are oprn from 9.00–6.00, Monday to Saturday, with a 24 hour message answering service. Email address: orders@bookpoint.co.uk

British Library Cataloguing in Publication Data
A catalogue record for this title is available from the British Library

ISBN 0 340 80199 9

First published 2001
Impression number   10 9 8 7 6 5 4 3 2 1
Year   2007 2006 2005 2004 2003 2002 2001

Copyright © 2001 John Townsend

Typeset by SX Composing DTP, Rayleigh, Essex
Printed in Great Britain for Hodder & Stoughton Educational, a division of Hodder Headline Plc, 338 Euston Road, London NW1 3BH by Redwood Books, Trowbridge, Wiltshire

Contents

Could an A.B.C. like this panther be roaming near your home?

1 A.B.C.

They call them A.B.C.s.
That means Alien Big Cats.
Some people say there could be
hundreds out there.
Some say they have seen big cats on the moors.
Some say A.B.C.s live wild in woods and fields,
or in the hills.
Some say they are on the loose closer to home.

A.B.C.s have been seen in parks and gardens
near towns.
But can big cats really be on the prowl
just a few miles away?
Could you meet a lion face to face
while walking your dog?

Wait till you read some of the facts.
You might think twice before going for a hike.
If you go down to the woods today,
beware of a big surprise . . .

2 In the News

For years, newspapers have told
of strange animals –
big cats in the middle of open spaces.

WAS SHEEP KILLED BY PUMA?

MAN SEES PANTHER LEAP GATE

LEOPARDS RAID BINS AT NIGHT

Headlines like these
have been in papers all over Britain.
Other news stories are even more shocking . . .

BIG CATS STALK THE MOORS

**FARMERS TELL OF WILD BEASTS OUT THERE
IN THE DARK**

BITE MARKS POINT TO SAVAGE KILLER

This is a true report from a newspaper in 1999:

Police have begun a tiger hunt in Yorkshire.
A fork-lift truck driver told
of meeting a large and muddy cat-like animal
while he was working on a farm.
He had to dive on to the floor of his cab
as the large orange and black striped cat
stood up on its hind legs,
snarling and lashing out with its claws.

He said, 'It jumped on to its back legs and
took a few swipes at me as I sat in the cab.
I could see its mouth open wide and
its claws looked like razors.
It was a tiger – there is no doubt about it.'

Can such stories really be true?

3 Where did they come from?

There have been reports of big cats living wild
in the UK since the 1970s.
That was when farmers first found
dead farm animals.
That was when people took
the first fuzzy photos of cat shapes.

Some of the photos were hoaxes.
Many experts said it was all made up.
After all, how can big cats come all the way
across Europe from Africa?

In the 1960s,
it was common for pop stars
to own panthers or pumas.
They were signs of fame and wealth.
You could even buy leopards from
a big London store!

This A.B.C. was photographed in Zennor, Cornwall, in 1988. What do you think – a hoax or real?

But in 1974 a pet leopard changed it all.
It was being taken for a walk
down the Fulham Road in London
when it went mad.
It jumped on a young boy and killed him.
It was tragic.

In all the fuss that followed, the law was changed.
It was all done in a hurry
without much thought as to what might happen.
People with pet big cats had a problem.
They had to pay a lot of money for a licence.
Or pay an even bigger fine.
The animal would go to a zoo or be put down.

But there was another choice.
A panther could be put in the back of a Range Rover.
After a drive into the hills or woods after dark,
it would be simple.
It's easy to park in a lay-by and
leave the back door open.

Not long ago, there was a headline
In *The Times* newspaper.

Lion tamer says he freed big cats on the moors

The report told how a man who owned many big cats
let them all go.

He said, 'I know other people who did the same.
Twenty-six years ago, I let out a panther
on to the moors on the Pennines at Snake Pass.
It was miles from anywhere.
I've always been an animal lover.
I just couldn't put it down.'

The same news report said something else –
something that shocked a lot of people.

Big cat experts believe there could be
up to 100 panthers and pumas roaming free.
They are the offspring of beasts let free in the 1970s.
At that time, it was not illegal to release them.
Now that did put the cat among the pigeons!

This woman is walking her pet cheetah in London, 1939.

4   The Proof

Some animal experts have told strange stories.
They have found dead sheep
which have all the signs of being killed by big cats.
Leopard footprints have been found in mud
near to dead farm animals.

One expert said,
'I went into the wood
where a sheep had just been killed
and I heard the cough of a leopard
about 300 metres away.
That's a sound I heard many times
when I worked in zoos.
It cut through the wood like a knife.'

Every year people report to the police
that they have seen big cats.
There are still no clear photos.
No big cat has been caught yet.
But they have been reported
in most parts of the UK,
in parts of Europe and across the USA.

Cougars have often chased hikers in America.

Cougars (or mountain lions) have attacked
a few people in remote parts of America.
People have also seen big cats in Australia.
Most police forces now keep files
of the reports that come in every month.
Yet big cats are very good at keeping out of sight.
They hide from humans when they can.
They know how to keep out of the way.

Even the wild leopards in South Africa
that live in the townships keep well out of sight.
Hardly anyone sees them.
But they are still there –
hunting around homes after dark.

Big cats are experts at keeping out of the way.
Even so, now and again,
they give themselves away.
Late at night,
when they jump a hedge or cross a road,
they are seen in car headlights.
The proof they are out there
is when their eyes shine under a full moon.
Or when there's a low growl from the woods.

5 Reports

For many years,
the police have kept files on A.B.C.s.
When people report seeing big cats,
the details are noted.
Often the newspapers will tell the story.
Sometimes they make a big fuss and go over-the-top.
Yet each week
you can usually find a few lines in a local paper.
It may still make the news,
but sightings are not so rare now.

Here are some recent accounts.
They all come from this century.

HUNT FOR BIG CAT

A big cat was thought to have attacked a dog last night. A vet said the collie dog had wounds that were like the bites and claw marks of a very large cat.

Police also say that a man in the same area reported deep claw marks in his pine door. 'It looks as if a large animal tried to get in through the cat-flap,' he said. 'Big cats have been seen here before.'

Another report came within a few days.
It was in the same part of the country.

The black beast is back

A big black cat was seen leaping a tall fence today.
A witness said, 'I'm sure it's a black panther.
I saw them in South America when I was in the Army,
so I know just what they look like.
It was jet black, had a small head, long body and
A very long tail.'

This is just another in a long list of sightings
that are on the increase.

Big cat seen by pair

A man and wife saw a large cat-like animal
near their home this week.
They said,
'It moved like a big cat and it was a couple of feet high.
It was not a dog.
We saw it walk across the field by our house.'

None of these reports is very dramatic.
They are just like all the other reports
in newspapers each week.
But sometimes there is more to report.
Sometimes the big cats come too close for comfort.

6 Close Encounters

A man was out walking his dog.
It was early in the morning in winter.
He opened the gate to cross the lane next to his house.
There was a sound of running feet.
He thought it was a horse.

He looked behind and saw a black animal
like a large dog.
It ran straight at him.
He shouted and the animal ran off to the side,
just a few metres away.
It had a cat's head and a long tail.
It left a strong smell – like a tom cat.

It was a young panther – less than a year old.
It may have been out all night
marking its hunting ground.
Perhaps the man's dog made the panther run at him.
Or it may not have seen the man at all.
It ran off up the lane.
The man went home to phone the police.

There was another close encounter
one Saturday night in May.
It was on a housing estate.
A man woke early to hear a cry
outside his window.
He looked out to see a fox.
It was scared stiff.
Then a large black cat sped by.
It chased the fox up the road.
The man was sure it was a panther.

A railway line runs down the middle of this estate.
It seems that big cats use railway lines as paths.
So watch out for trains and A.B.C.s!

Someone saw this same panther
in the same town a few days later.
It walked slowly past a man in his car –
just a few metres away.
He also went to phone the police.

Maybe all of these people were wrong.
Perhaps they saw a dog or a very large pet cat.
What do YOU think?

7   How do they live?

You may think big cats like hot weather.
You may think they need to live in jungles
or in the African bush.
Some say that big cats can't live in the cold and wet.
Can they really live for long in the UK,
Europe or the USA?

The truth is – they can adapt.
The cold is no problem.
Nor is rain.
They like water!
Their thick coats are just right for our winters.
But can they really find enough food?
What do they eat?

Experts say there is plenty for them to find.
They will kill birds, rabbits, badgers,
foxes, deer and even fish.
They have been seen chasing squirrels.
And when they can't get those,
there are always farm animals.

Leopards are hard to see in long grass.

Cattle and sheep have been killed.
A.B.C.s have taken hens and lambs as well.
After all, they are expert hunters.
They can hide so well.
They are very clever at not being seen.

Big cats are known to hunt over a large area,
up to 200 square miles.
They hunt at night and rest during the day.
They sleep a lot.
They lie low in woods, in empty barns or caves.
They may hide in railway tunnels in the day.

Even in Africa, where there are many big cats,
they are not often seen.
They are skilled at keeping well out of sight.
They are masters of surprise.
Even some native tribes in Africa
have never seen big cats –
but they are still there.
They can see us – but can we see them?

8   The Main Suspects

Lions or tigers on the loose would be bad news!
The main suspects are the puma,
the leopard and the lynx.

Pumas are brown with white on their faces.
They can be 1.5 m long
and about 75 cm tall at the shoulder.
An adult puma can weight up to 100 kg
(over 15 stone).

They come from North and South America.
The name puma means 'silent killer'.
They have been known to attack people.
Other names for the puma are mountain lion
or cougar.

They can travel up to 25 miles in a day.
Like many big cats, pumas can swim.
They can cross rivers.
They tend to hunt at dawn and dusk.

Leopards are slimmer cats.
They can be light brown with spots
or black all over.

Leopards leap down onto any passing prey.

These are called black panthers.
They can swim and will eat fish.
A leopard kills with a bite to the neck of its prey.

It often drops down on to its kill from a tree.
It tends to sleep and eat in trees.
Leopards come from Africa
but have been seen in the middle of Britain
by railway lines – asleep in the sun!

The lynx is a smaller cat with tufts on its ears.
It is used to cold weather as it comes from Canada.
It is just as much at home in the hills and
gardens of Europe.

Big cats on the loose have been seen with cubs.
It is even thought these cats have cross-bred.
Maybe pumas have bred with panthers.

If these big cats are breeding in the wild,
who knows how many will survive.
Perhaps they will soon become a common sight
in our woods and fields!

It might be useful to know what to do
if you meet one face to face.

The lynx is used to cold weather.

9 What to do if you meet one

Are there really so many big cats
out there in our countryside?
If so, what can we do?
Will people get hurt?
Can the police do much?
Will an A.B.C. pop up in your back garden?
There may be a risk of danger
but the last thing we want is mass panic.

Remember that big cats are fast, powerful
and hard to see.
If you go out looking for a big cat,
you are sure not to see one!
But if you are out for a hike in wild country,
it may be wise to keep on the look-out.

Here are a few tips to follow
if you ever meet a big cat face to face:

- If a big cat is straight in front of you,
  back away slowly.
- Never run away and
  never turn your back on it.
- Do not make sudden moves or noise.
- If you have a dog with you, get it on a lead.
  Keep it under control.
  A dog may attract a big cat to you.
- Do not stare a big cat in the eyes.
  This will be seen as a threat and it may attack.
- If the big cat walks away from you,
  keep still and quiet till it has gone.

Only if a big cat runs at you, should you hit out.
If it gets angry and looks like it will charge,
you must do these things:

- Try to make yourself look big
  by moving out your arms.
  Open your coat wide.
  Make yourself as tall as you can.
- Try to find a stick to pick up – just in case.
- Stay in a close group, if you are with others.

By now a big cat is more likely to back away.
If it does leap at you,
you must try to do the following:

- Make a lot of noise.
  Scream.
  Blowing a whistle will be even better.
- Throw sticks or stones at it –
  but keep that big stick with you!
- Hit out and fight back.
  A big cat does not expect its prey to fight.
  The shock may scare it off.
- Use that stick.
  Try to prod the cat's nose.
  They hate it!
- Kick, stamp, flap a coat, shout,
  throw mud, punch.
- BUT DON'T RUN!

The chances of any of this happening are very small.
Pumas and panthers don't like to attack people
unless they have to.
But if a farmer takes a pot shot
at a big cat and hurts it,
we are all in danger.
A wounded leopard can be a real threat.
That's when we might have a man-eater
on the doorstep!

10 A matter of time

Some say it is only a matter of time
until the first big cat is caught.
Then everyone will know the truth –
that they are out there.
Some say it is only a matter of time
until someone is hurt by a big cat on the loose.
Then there will be a big fuss.
Some say it is only a matter of time
until the whole subject is shown to be a big hoax.
Then it will all be forgotten.

Whatever happens,
there will be many more false alarms.
There will be more over-the-top news stories.
There will be more fuss and scare stories.
But there may be more proof.
These stories won't go away yet.

If there are really big cats out there,
they may keep breeding.
A lot more may roam our countryside
in a few years.

On the other hand,
they may begin to die out after a while.
The stories may pass into myth and legend.
Who knows?
What do you think?

If you want to find out more,
try looking at the Internet.
You may see more about recent sightings.
You may change your mind.

Try looking at
http://www.ukbigcats.tsx.org/
or
http://www.webalias.com/cryptozoology

Soon we may learn far more. After all, it's just a
matter of time . . .